SELFIES WITH
KOMODOS

For my two talented daughters – Karen & Linette
B.M.

For the amazing children and staff
at Seymour Primary Academy
E.B.

Text copyright © Brian Moses 2023
Illustrations copyright © Ed Boxall 2023
First published in Great Britain and in the USA in 2023
by Otter-Barry Books, Little Orchard, Burley Gate,
Herefordshire, HR1 3QS
www.otterbarrybooks.com

A catalogue record for this book is available
from the British Library

Designed by Arianna Osti

ISBN 978-1-91307-409-8

Illustrated with a mixture of pen and pencil,
paint and digital media

Printed in Great Britain

9 8 7 6 5 4 3 2 1

SELFIES WITH KOMODOS

POEMS BY BRIAN MOSES

ILLUSTRATED BY Ed Boxall

Otter-Barry BOOKS

Contents

Not on a Train

How often have you travelled on a train and heard
a phone ring?
How often does the person holding the phone start
the conversation with, "Hello, it's me, I'm on a train!"?
But what if you weren't?

"Hello, it's me, I'm not on a train,
I'm riding a horse towards the mountains of Spain.
I'm in New York walking my chihuahua,
I'm on a camel crossing the Sahara.
I'm beneath the waves in a yellow submarine,
I'm lounging with a rock star in a stretch limousine.
I'm ascending and descending in an ancient
    elevator,
I'm confined to my cabin in a rusty cargo freighter.
I'm clinging to an asteroid hurtling through space,
I'm with Dr Who, without time or place.
I'm a cruise ship stowaway somewhere at sea,
I'm an eighteen-wheeler's hitchhiker, feeling really
    free.
I'm on the lip of Grand Canyon in my rented
    Winnebago,
on a trip to find myself in downtown San Diego.
It's the truth, I tell you, I just had to explain
all the reasons why I'm not on a train."

I'm a Cat

I'm a cat on the wall
caterwauling,
a **cat**astrophe cat
always falling.
I'm a **cat**egory cat
classified first class,
I'm a **cat**nap cat
asleep on the grass.
I'm a **cat**erpillar cat
stalking a mouse,
a **cat**aclysmic cat
chaotic in the house.
I'm a **cat**apult cat
moving in for a kill,
I'm a **cat**'s-eye cat
looking for a thrill.
I'm a **cat**ty cat
spiteful and mean,
a **cat**walk cat
in my own limousine.
I'm a **cat**call cat
with a swift reply,
a **cat**'s whisker cat
to dogs passing by.
But one thing I'm not
is a **cat**tery cat,
so don't you ever
think about that!

Romeo's Nine Lives

Life Number Nine was a run up a tree,
somehow missed my footing coming down,
slipped and fell through branches
to the ground. Did that body twist
cats do, to land safe and sound.

Number Eight was the jaws of a dog
and could have meant death,
had I not achieved the kind of
climb-down most cats disapprove of.
Simply spun round, turned tail and ran.

Seven was the fault of a boy and a bike,
a pizza delivery one Sunday night.
Fast asleep I failed to hear
the bike arrive, just woke in time,
leapt clear.

Six found me hunting rats in a shed,
got locked in, starved, half-dead,
ate spiders, flies, and fortunately
someone heard my weakening cries.

Life Number Five was lost for love
when I thought I'd met my Juliet.
She led me a dance and I failed
to see some monster truck intent
on flattening me.

Four saw me ambushed by Scooby Doo,
the kind of dog you don't want to meet.
Left one of my claws attached to his cheek
and deep scratches down his jaws.

Life Number Three I lost recently
when I rested on the bedroom window sill
and a chain saw powered up next door,
I screeched and fell two floors.

Number Two, a hullabaloo,
a cacophony, a pack of dogs.
I ran like I'd never run before,
got clipped by a car, limped back
to my door.

And now, with only one life to lose,
I think I'll lie in the sun
and just snooze!

Selfies with Komodos

You'd better not take a selfie
with the dragon they call Komodo
or Hocus-Pocus, Diplodocus,
you'll be more dead than a dodo.

He won't be a photo in your family book
even if you ask him nicely.
The look he gives you shouldn't be ignored,
his expression is simply icy.

He won't be your dancing partner
in your holiday video,
he can't be tamed and ridden
in some wild west rodeo.

It's no good trying to persuade him,
he's always in a bad mood,
and don't call round when he's eating,
asking to share his food.

It's senseless to risk being headless
when he closes his mighty jaws
or find that you're suddenly swiped
by a flick from his wicked claws.

Oh, Komodo, no, Komodo,
if what I hear is true,
nothing but another Komodo
should risk getting close to you.

The Possibility of Dragons

Ricky was sure he'd seen dragon prints,
clearly marked on the stretch of damp sand
between high and low water.
They were nothing like he'd ever seen before.
He had no idea there were dragons on the
shoreline.

They must be fresh, he thought,
looking round and shivering.
He'd have to search through
The Boys' Book of Dragons,
try to find what breed they might be.

It wasn't every day he found evidence of dragons,
he'd better look out too, for scorch marks and tail
tracks.
If dragons were coming back
he wanted to be the first to find out.

He'd be famous,
on the news, being interviewed.
Bit of a disappointment though to viewers,
"I didn't actually see the dragon, just its tracks."

"What good are tracks?" they'd ask.
"We need photos, video footage,
fire and flames."
"Give us evidence," they'd say.
"Then we'll believe you."

So Ricky went searching, turning over rocks,
looking into caves. This was something to fill
the idle hours, the best quest he'd ever had.
He'd find them, he counted on that.
The world would be empty, and far less
interesting, if the possibility of dragons
once more went up in smoke.

Dragons

When I met the dragon of vanity
we gazed into his mirror.

When I met the dragon of discovery
we roamed the known world together.

When I met the dragon of imagination
we tiptoed in and out of each other's dreams.

When I met the dragon of loneliness
we shared his cave.

When I met the dragon of doom
he spoke to me of worlds ending.

When I met the dragon of destiny
my fate was sealed.

A Plea from the Rescue Centre for Mythical Beasts

One or two of our mythical creatures
have proved very hard to rehome.
Nobody wants a Gorgon
whose stare could turn them to stone.

But a dragon below the floorboards
will provide you with underfloor heating.
Many heads of a Hydra will watch
from each window while you're sleeping.

Roars from a Centaur will also help
to keep away burglars too.
And a Cyclops will always say
that he's keeping his eye on you.

A Banshee's high-pitched shriek
will wake you from your sleep
better than any alarm clock,
if your sleep is heavy and deep.

Cerberus, the three-headed dog,
will cause a stir in the park,
warning off rival dogs
with his fearsome bark, bark, bark.

Some creatures we can't get enough of,
like the popular Unicorn,
and everyone wants to rehome
a lucky Leprechaun.

An Ogre for classroom discipline
would be of assistance to teachers.
So won't you help us rehome
one of our mythical creatures?

What if Pandora Had Never Opened the Box?

What if she'd been cautious
instead of curious?

What if she'd hesitated,
sought advice first?

What if she'd been quicker
to slam down the lid?

If something had tried to escape
she might have prevented it.

Imagine a world where
sadness, misery, disease
had never been unleashed.

Imagine a world released
from darkness and death.

A world where joy and happiness,
love and wonder
have no limits.

Oh Pandora, what did you do?

Looks like all our worries and fears
are simply down to you.

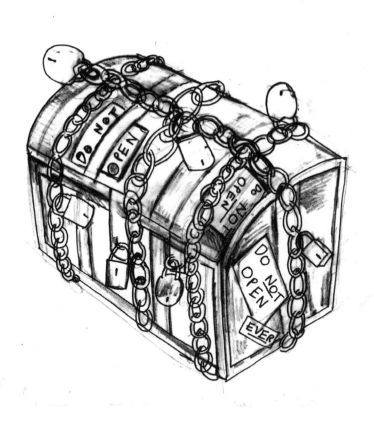

Learning to Fly

I'm learning to fly,
taking lessons from the birds,
watching landings and take-offs,
stealing secrets from the gulls:
how to glide on currents of air,
how to lift and float and hover.

I'm learning from the swifts and the martins
how to feed while I'm in flight.
I'm learning from the jackdaws
that nest in our chimneys,
learning from the blackbirds,
their chat and communication.

I'm learning the physics and aerodynamics
I didn't learn in school.
Learning migration from
long-distance travellers,
having navigational conversations
with wandering albatrosses.

I'm learning too, from the dragonflies,
the nimbleness needed to stay aloft,
from the bees and the butterflies –
I'm adding their skills
to my store of knowledge.

Till one day I'll take off into the sky,
I'll soar and I'll dive, flutter and float.
No need for airlines or jumbo jets,
I'll cross the seas all by myself,
like a boat in an ocean of cloud.

How great to see everyone stare,
to feel their envy, hear questions
tumbling from their lips,
knowing how easily I could slip away
and never return.

Freezing Time

I'd like to freeze time…

when I'm on a roller-coaster ride,
held for a moment at the very top
and about to lock into
that downward rush.

I'd like to freeze time…

when it's Christmas Day.
Maybe time could play tricks
and elasticate the hours,
so when I think it's over,
it lets me relive it again.

I'd like to freeze time…

at the moment just after
I score the winning goal
for my team,
the endless congratulations,
the continuous roars of approval
would be mine for a long time.

I'd like to freeze time…
so my puppy never grows up,
my holidays never end,
my birthday presents take forever
to open and
my Maths test never happens.

But then I could find
that I'm eternally a school-child,
or the weather stays cold
and never gets warm,
or a storm constantly rages overhead,
or I stay awake all the time
and never get to bed,
or I can't leave the supermarket,
ever.

Maybe it's all for the best
if time ticks on
as it's always done.

Remarkable Names

If I'd been given the name of Hugh Pugh
I'd have changed it, wouldn't you?

If I was called Ima Hog or Newton Hooton,
Luscious Pea or Bambina Broccoli,
I'd have kicked up a heck of a fuss.

Horace Clutch would have been too much to bear
and anyone wearing metal should ignore the pull
of Miss Magnetic Love.

B Brooklyn Bridge was too much of a stretch
and Welcome Baby Darling just too cute.

But some names must have been just right:
the chorister Justin Tune, Miss Screech
the singing teacher, Plummer & Leek,
popular plumbers and Wire and Tapping
from the New York City police.

But no one would have blamed
Appendicitis Laryngitis Meningitis Peritonitis
    Tonsilitis Jackson
if he'd left home as soon as he could
and never set eyes on his parents again.

*The names included here are all real, verified names,
and feature in the book 'Remarkable Names of Real People'
compiled by John Train.*

Clouds

I'd like to lounge around
on a sofa of beaches

looking up at
a ceiling of clouds.

Just as I did as a kid,
I'd lie on my back
and stare at the sky,

try to find faces
in the passing shapes
of clouds.

I'd find my family,
my uncles, aunts and cousins.

I'd find my teacher's face
in a stern-looking
cumulonimbus.

I'd see kings and queens
and wonder what they were doing
flying over my town.

My dog too, looking down on me,
chasing the puffy clouds
as they rolled along.

I'd wonder what it would be like
to wander among clouds,

to change their direction,
move the big black ones away
to rain on some other town.

These were the angry ones,
bursting to loosen the rage
inside them.

Others were gentle strollers,
drifting to destinations
I could only dream of.

Some were airships,
dragons, covered wagons
crossing the plains of sky.

Some were lonesome,
single puffs of cloud,
left behind like
lost children.

I'd stare and I'd stare
till my neck began to ache
and the horizon tilted,
making me giddy.

Clouds were there for me
when life was drab,
filling my imagination
with wisps of wonder.

Diamonds

There are diamonds hiding here,
reflections beneath the sea's surface.

So I'm kicking at the water,
releasing
a spray of diamonds
on a sunny day.

I'm kicking at the water,
persuading
the sea to relinquish
its treasure.

Kick harder,
it's a torrent,
harder still and
it's a waterfall.

As it ebbs and flows,
the diamonds roll
and whatever I uncover
slides through my fingers,
slips from my hands.

Hard to accept
these diamonds are not forever.

The Sea's Ghosts

Written after visiting the cemetery overlooking the sea in
Whitby where many former whalers & fishermen are buried.
It struck me, when I was there on a particularly windswept
day, that the sea was calling them back.

In the days of the saints and the fisher folk,
The whaling boats and the jet mines,
The sea's voice could be heard
Through the surging of the storm.

You could hear it call
To the sad ones on the cliffs,
To the lost ones in the sea,
To the broken ones
In the cemetery:

Follow me now, as you once
Followed me…

And the voices in the breakers,
The wailing from the wind,

The beckoning curve of
A cresting wave,
Still calling.

Sometimes it's a murmur,
Sometimes a command.

In the singing of the sea,
In the gabble of the gulls,
In the sighing and
The stillness

In the whispers as you pass
From the graves in the grass...

What was once,

Is now,

Will be.

Underwater Magicians

Recently I heard
of underwater magicians
conjuring up shoals of fish
letting them leap into the night sky
and hang there as stars.

And when they weren't busy with fish
they'd unlock the memories
of molluscs
discover how once they were
soft pillows where mermaids
might rest their heads.

These same magicians would extract
secrets from the mouths
of drowned sailors
and teach sea shanties
to choirs of crabs.

But best of all
were the stories they'd tell
of sea horses
rummaging through the blankets
of the ocean's bed
for the smiles that fall from rainbows.

Whalentine

If we were whales
we'd cause a commotion
leaping in and out of the ocean.
We'd harmonise as we floated along
serenading each other in songs
that broadcast our love for hundreds of miles
while I bathed in the warmth of your whale smiles.
We'd spend our time in the warmest seas
with baby whales to cuddle and tease.
I'd be a blue whale but I'd never be blue
as long as I wandered the oceans with you.

But I know this would only be a dream
and nothing is ever as good as it seems.
Life in the sea, for me, would be grim
as sadly, regrettably, I never learnt to swim.

Labrador

My dog's a sweetie,
she's labradorable.

Loves her food,
she's labradicted.

In her teenage years
she was
labradolescent.

She draws
with her claws,
she's a labradoodler.

My dog's magic,
she's a labracadabrador.

I love my dog,
I labradore her.

My Dog's Bucket List

Sniff deeply and lengthily
all the smells I'm denied
when my human and I
walk the village street.

Sample as many varieties
of cowpat as I can
to check that I've completed
my culinary tour of
the cow field.

Roll luxuriously in fox scat
then be allowed to enjoy the smell
as it matures, instead of being
immediately hosed down.

Bark, bark, bark till
I can bark no more
when that noisy delivery driver
slams his fist against
our door.

Stare at the doggy treats on the shelf
for long enough and hard enough
till the force of my stare
brings them crashing to the floor.

Practise my ducking and diving
till I'm in tip-top shape
just in case next door's cat
decides on fight instead of flight.

Then finally, show that
good-for-nothing cat
who rules this neighbourhood.

Although at my age now I'm realising
I ought to be more creative
it's time I started to think
outside the (dog biscuit) box.

Nobody Told the Dog

Nobody told the dog
that his dog days were numbered,
that he'd only got two months
at most, or so the vet said.
Nobody told him to take to his bed,
to unleash the demons of worry
and let them scrabble about in his head.

The dog's days were still fine,
just some aches and pains, a tightness
in his chest, but the dog did
what he'd always done,
enjoyed his food, his walks
and now and then broke into a run.

Nobody told the dog
he was fighting a losing battle.
He lay in his sunny spot on the floor,
kept one eye on next door's cat,
enjoyed the attention, the extra fuss.
And everyone knew that seven
months later he really should have been gone.

But nobody told the dog
and the dog
lived on.

Some Days

Some days stride out
and knock you down
before you even set foot
outside the door.

Other days wait in ambush
with something set to detonate
under your feet.

Some days eye you up
and follow you round
like a homeless dog
tagging your heels.

Some days are like spies,
checking up on everything you do,
surprising you on corners,
quickly disappearing down alleyways
as you turn.

Some days clout you,
shout out, 'Wanna fight?'

But the best ones, the special ones
and sometimes even the
nothing-special ones,
just wrap themselves around you
gradually, comfortingly...

and give you a gentle squeeze.

please show me a pathway that stretches to
    the stars.

Instead of a mobile phone
please teach me the language I need to help me
    speak with angels.

Instead of a computer
please reveal to me the mathematics of meteors
    and motion.

Instead of the latest computer game
please come with me on a search for dragons in
    the wood behind our house.

Instead of an e-reader
please read to me from a book of ancient
knowledge.

Instead of a digital camera
please help me remember faces and places,
mystery and moonbeams.

Instead of a 3D TV
please take me to an empty world that I can people
with my imagination.

Instead of electronic wizardry
please show me how to navigate the wisdom
inside me.

Librarians

Librarians hold keys
to places only they can take us.

They know where to look
to find the landscapes we long
to explore, and those
we've yet to discover.

They know where to hide
from anything that frightens us,

where to move forward
and when to step back.

They know where treasure
can be found,

where to discover the pieces
of puzzles we strive so hard
to complete.

They know magic, or if they don't,
they know where to find
the ones who do.

They are trained to travel in time,
to lay down stepping stones,
to put in place bridges.

They are detectives, prospectors,
collectors of knowledge,
explorers, deliverers,
builders of dreams,

and always, always
much more than they seem.

There are secrets
only librarians know,

until they show us.

Lost in a Book

I'm lost in a book…

I'm shaking off snow in the forests of Narnia.

I'm with Lyra on the back of a great white bear.

I'm rambling with the Famous Five
and climbing the Faraway Tree.

I'm playing quidditch (but not very well)
in the skies above Hogwarts.

I'm wandering in Wonderland with Alice.

I'm sitting with the Boy at the Back of the Class.

I'm leading a War Horse to safety
with explosions in our ears.

I'm with Barney teaching Stig how to open tins.

I'm looking through the wrong end
of Rebecca's telescope.

I'm in a lighthouse writing letters.

I'm finding an angel in a garden shed.

I'm training a dragon, meeting Mr Tom,
spinning a web for Charlotte.

I'm with Carrie, with Tyke,
with Captain Hook....

Yes, I'm lost in a book
but please don't try to find me.

I've actually found
that lost in a book
is exactly where I want to be.

Haunted Furniture

Apparently there is a brisk trade in haunted furniture.

I seem to be host to a ghost
Having bought an old chair
On eBay.

No sooner had it been delivered
Than a chill seemed to
Hang around it.

No one could sit in it for long
Without feeling cold,
Without starting to shiver.

The cat who slept anywhere
Wouldn't go near it.
There was fear in his eyes.

The dog slunk past it,
Ears back, tail down,
No wriggle of a wag.

Silence intensified
When the room was empty,
But it felt like someone was there.

"I've heard of these things," a friend said.
"Had a bed once where I couldn't sleep.
The nightmares were relentless."

"Wear red," I read.
"If you live in fear of ghosts
It will scare them away."

But the room grew colder.
When I blew out my breath
It was visible in the air.

I sold the chair, didn't tell,
But banging doors and footsteps
Told me the ghost had stayed on.

"Why me?" I asked myself,
The house sold, door closed
For the final time.

But footsteps followed me down the path,
And a chill voice whispered,
"You're mine."

Vampire Facial

Smear that blood around your lips
Rub it in with my fingertips
Quickly give your neck a nip

You'll love my vampire facial

I yearn to hear your breathless hiss
Feel the touch of your sharp kiss
Being close is such sweet bliss

You'll love my vampire facial

Look at me, I'm sabre-tooth
My bite is lethal, that's the truth
Old as time, but I need your youth

You'll love my vampire facial

Such delight if you stay with me
You'll love my witty repartee
Be mine for all eternity

You'll love my vampire facial

And although my smile is glacial
My castle is quite palatial
Your room would be so spatial

When you book my vampire facial.

Night Train to Transylvania

On the night train to Transylvania
you can
check out groovy graveyards you may have missed
on previous trips.
You can talk to estate agents about buying
your very own mausoleum
where you'll sleep soundly by day
and then easily escape from at night.
Discuss with other like-minded creatures
the best ways to frighten victims,
how to trick them to bare their necks.
Learn different types of bites
and which will give you the deepest drink.
Discover the comfiest coffins
in which to lie for all eternity.
Be warned in advance of the tricks and
    paraphernalia
of the vampire hunter, of the ways to combat garlic
and avoid a sharpened stake.
You'll meet and mingle with many denizens
of the darkest night, with ghouls and gremlins,
werewolves and warlocks.

So be warned,
that little old lady might be Grand High Witch,
that buffet car attendant could easily
be Count Dracula's descendant
and even that hairy porter could be Voldermort
(just don't speak his name),
on the night train to Transylvania.

Reasons Why Your Train Was Late This Morning

The train on Platform One
had a note from its mum.

The train on Platform Two
went up in a puff of smoke,
someone said *you know who* was on board.
Don't say his name,
it may not be a joke.

The train on Platform Three
stopped for a cup of tea,
a sandwich, a cake and two bags of crisps,
then went for a dip in the sea.

The train that should have been on Platform Four
found a secret door to another dimension,
now it's millions of light years away.

The train on Platforms Five, Six and Seven
came in sideways.

You missed the train on Platform Eight,
it left already, you were late.

The Moment

You can never stand on too many bridges,
watching the water slipping beneath,
seeing the salmon leaping upstream
while the sun dips into the forest.

You can never stare at too many sunsets,
seeing the orange merge with the red,
watching the purple hues drip down
in a canvas of colour.

You can never take too many journeys,
twisting and turning on mountain tracks,
hiking to lakes where the ice
is spider-webbed with cracks.

You can never pause on too many towpaths,
gazing at myriad reflections.
You can never explore too many castles,
hearing echoes from the past
in every footstep.

You can never shuffle through sand on too many
    beaches,
stopping to wonder where you are
and how time has been hour-glassed away.

You can never stop and stare for too long....

It's that stopping and looking and thinking
and feeling and wondering...

a moment that no photograph can capture.

Be aware,
be wise,
catch the moment.

Things I Haven't Seen Enough Of...

A chain poem

Waterfalls that cascade down mountains
Mountains made red by sunsets
Sunsets that fade to a soft glowing sky
Sky seen from skylights in the heads of houses
Houses that float and ripple reflectively in streams
Streams that dawdle their way down hillsides
Hillsides that arch their backs below clouds
Clouds that hover and hang above waterfalls

Custodian

I am a custodian.
Custodian of the landscape,
its mysteries and memories.

Custodian of the May blossom
that wakes the hedges
after winter slumbers.

Custodian of languages:
the calling of cattle at first light,
the arguments of foxes,
the complaining of sheep,
the gossip from overhead geese.

Custodian of the berries and sloes,
the rich bounty of hedgerows,
of the fallen trees,
the scampering of squirrels,
the whirring of pheasants' wings,
the hide-and-seek deer,
the woodpecker's drum roll.

Custodian of winter's snow and summer's drought,
of sunset and sunrise, of misty hideaways,
of dripping fog, of woods and streams,
the valleys, hills and skies.

I am a custodian.
I have no desire to own these things,
these places, just to know
that on my watch,
and until I relinquish responsibility,

all is as it should be.

Stay Clear of Flip-Flop Creatures

Words like hurly-burly and dilly-dally are known as
'flip-flop' words

Don't run around with a hurly-burly,
it always wants to be somewhere early,
huffing and puffing, twisty and twirly,
you'd best keep clear of a hurly-burly.

A fuddy-duddy is something you'll hate,
old-fashioned, somewhat out-of-date.
And don't make a dilly-dally your mate,
it will always delay you, leaving you late.

If you make friends with a fiddle-faddle,
you'll be up the creek without a paddle.
It will mess up your mind, your brain it will addle,
my advice would be stay clear, skedaddle.

The hustle-bustle will drive you wild,
it will be your unwelcome, mischievous child.
It will never be something meek and mild
but an untamed nuisance, forever reviled.

A razzle-dazzle will shine in your eyes
but out of his trickster's mouth tumble lies.
And lovey-dovey is quite a surprise,
you could be trapped before you realise.

You won't make sense of a mumbo-jumbo,
whatever it says you won't comprehend.
Your world will just turn topsy-turvy
if you make a flip-flop creature your friend.

Oh, What a Day!

Written after hearing about Dragon Awareness Day and National Unicorn Day.

It's Outrageously Coloured Pants day.
It's Do Acrobatics with Ants day.

It's Dance with your Dog on the Duvet day.
It's Wear Wellington Boots for your Ballet day.

It's Invite a Woodlouse to your House day.
It's Making Music with a Mouse day.

It's Bend a Banana the Other Way day.
It's Teaching Crocodiles to Play Croquet day.

It's Abseiling Down from Wheelie Bins day.
It's Long-jumping over Baked-bean Tins day.

It's Follow your Nose to a Rose day.
It's Learn Disco-dancing with Dominoes day.

It's Do as you Please with a Sneeze day.
It's Walk to the Shops on your Knees day.

It's Playing Billiards with Bears day.
It's Tobogganing Down Stairs day.

It's Make a Movie of your Dreams day.
It's Nothing Is Quite Like It Seems day.

*Now add to this list and turn it into a really long poem

Words

I wonder how many words I've spoken
in my lifetime.

Words we say to each other every day,
the simple words *Hello*, *Goodbye*.
Words that comfort and caress,
the *Love You* words we wrap around ourselves,
the cosy words we cuddle up to.

All the words I've spoken to my dog
that she's only minimally understood,
all the promises I've made and broken,
even the words I've thought, but left unspoken.

There were words that ran away from me,
that I should have kept control of,
hateful words, spiteful words,
words I wished I could have reeled back in
the moment they escaped from my mouth.

Words that made a splash, words that dashed
from me to you, words too easily loosened,
words I regret, words that flew into a rage.
Words I picked off the page and threw away,
watching them wriggle along the ground.
Horrid things, squirmy things that lay there
till I picked them up again.

There were words I've spoken to myself,
words the size of boulders
that I couldn't get past my teeth.
Words that dawdled,
that balanced on the tip of my tongue
and then dropped like stones into water.

I wonder how many words? Would they fill
a jar, a barrel, a lake, an ocean?
Would they all get along
if I assembled them again,
like pieces of a jigsaw, coming together
then falling into place?
Or would they argue, fight, take flight once more?

Would the poems I've spoken unravel,
Would words I've used for so many years
desert me now when I need them most?
Would words become ghosts...

and could I suddenly find one day,
that scarily, spookily,
I have nothing more to say?

Taking Umbrage

Feeling offended or resentful

Too many times I've taken umbrage.

I've taken it to a football match
and railed at the referee.

I've taken it on a train, plonked it down
on the seat beside me, then moaned
when I had to shift it so someone
could sit down.

I've carried it to the library,
hoping I'd find a home for it
in the anger-management section.

I've taken it to the cinema,
where I've scoffed and thrown scorn
at actors on the screen.

I've trudged to school, brimful of umbrage,
and found it hard to hold down the lid.

I've hurled it away
and then found it waiting for me again.

I've felt it creep up on me, encircle me
till I find it hard to breathe.

I'm thinking now
that if I left my umbrage out in the rain

the wind might blow it away,
a fox might sneak off with it,
a dog might chew it up and swallow it.

And maybe then I'd no longer be
encumbered with umbrage…

and have no need to take it

anywhere.

Walking Wounded

At the end of each break-time
there's a row of the wounded
retired from the playground's hurly-burly
and waiting for the school's First-Aider
to take a look at whatever's cut,
whatever aches, what's bumped
or knocked.
Headaches, stomach aches,
aching toes, bloodied noses,
scratched cheeks, feeling faint,
feeling weak.

And everyone's hoping it's Mrs McVie
with her soothing words
and her tubs of cream
spread thickly to take the hurt away,
the silly rhymes that she says
like magic charms to banish pain.

But when it's Mrs Barker
with a voice that rumbles
like an imminent tsunami,
who bellows out
DON'T BOTHER ME IF IT'S JUST SCRATCHED
OR PATCHED – ONLY IF IT'S DETACHED...

the line dissolves,
children slip away,
knowing that sympathy can't be found
on such stony ground.

A Battle House of Flowers

In the town of Battle, East Sussex, close to where I live, there
used to be a flower shop called The Battle House of Flowers.

It's a battle house of flowers
where daffodils slog it out with dahlias,
you can hear their trumpets sound
the battle cry.
In this situation
even primroses strike
warlike poses, and there's no room
for shrinking violets
in a battle house of flowers.

Hyacinths and tulips
come out fighting,
while nobody focuses on
bad-tempered crocuses
setting up traps to topple
unwary sunflowers.

In a battle house of flowers
pansies are mugged by marigolds,
azaleas wail at lilies that threaten
to kill them, while geraniums hide
as the carnage continues.

No surprises, after all
there have always been
fighting flowers,
a tradition that began
centuries ago
with the Wars of the Roses.

*The Wars of the Roses (1455–1487) were civil wars fought
between the Houses of Lancaster and York. Their emblems
were roses, red for Lancaster and white for York.*

Postcards from Pluto

You know how happy I'd be
if you sent me
postcards from Pluto.

I've got postcards from Brighton
and Tenerife,
and ones from Australia's
Barrier Reef.

And one that you sent me
that glitters like stars.

But what I need, and I know you know,
is not something tawdry from
Venus or Mars,
just one or two postcards from Pluto.

You see, I think that
you're out of this world,
a planetary sparkle,
a space-travel girl.

There's a moon in your eyes,
stars dangle from your ears.
Your words excite me like
meteorite showers.

I'd like to be with you
wherever you go,
on your secret missions
in space.

But if that proves impossible,
make my heart glow
with one or two
postcards from Pluto.

Marathon Fit

Decided I'm not marathon fit
so I won't be pounding the streets of London
this year. Instead I'll be showing
a certain amount of empathy
by...

Walking my dog at a faster pace
than I usually do,

cleaning my teeth with a speedy
rather than an easy action,

improving on the number of circuits
I can do around our sofa
before collapsing onto the cushions,

thinking about taking a 100-metre hike
to the village shop to buy a paper,

attempting to peel an apple
in less than 5.4 seconds,

lifting cups of tea to my mouth
and then down again in a
streamlined and rhythmical motion,

while my dog too
will be turning around in her basket
more times than usual
before finding a comfortable position.

Marathon fit?

Not one bit.

Fallen Star

'Catch a falling star and put it in your pocket,
save it for a rainy day.'

When the conversation falters
and no one know what to say next,
that's when I reach into my pocket
and bring out my fallen star.

Then everybody oohs and aahs
like they do at firework displays.

"Where did you get it?"
they ask.
"How did you get it?"
they question.

But like a journalist
who never reveals his sources,
I keep the location to myself.
I don't want everyone finding fallen stars,
I don't want everyone stealing my secret.

It's the envy of everyone,
and for me,
the answer to everything.

It's the hope pulled from
hopelessness,
the light beyond darkness,
the joy after sadness.

My fallen star reveals
just what I am,
when I look into its heart,
its inner core.

And I value it,
I polish it often,
shine it, shape it,
keep it safe

for those inevitable
rainy days.

The Safe Side

I like to stay on the safe side.

Drink my tea cool and not hot.
Never think I'm anything I'm not.

Be careful when I cross the street.
Make sure I keep control of my feet.

Never skate on ice in case it cracks,
never explore the wrong side of the tracks.

Never step down onto a ledge
or walk too near a cliff edge.

Whenever I think I might
take a walk on the wild side,

the safe side pulls me back.

Earwig Corner

This is the name of a road junction near Lewes in East Sussex.

I think I've discovered
What happens round
Earwig Corner

It's always a crush, earwigs in a rush
Giving each other the brush-off
Round Earwig Corner

A scurry of earwigs
Always in a hurry
Round Earwig Corner

Schemers, dreamers, freedom fighters
A football team - Earwigs United
Round Earwig Corner

A blur, a flash, a dash of earwig
A smash and grab raid, a parade
Round Earwig Corner

Earwigs doing earwiggy things
Zipping between the fauna and flora
Round Earwig Corner

And earwigs too
Have taken over this poem
You'll notice an earwig bonanza
In every stanza

Storms

I feel sorry for the people
who'll never see
a storm that bears their name.

It would take an extensive,
never-ending storm season
to usher in storms
where there'd be a reason
for naming them X. Y or Z.

Unfair that it's always ABC,
although this year,
when the weather got worse
and conditions grew wetter,
we got as far as
Lorenzo, via George
and Henrietta.

Be fair to alphabet stragglers.
Let's name the next storm
Zak or Xander,
roller-coaster our way from end
to beginning.

Let Zoe come forward
from the back of the queue,
hijack the next storm
that batters through.

Then claim it and name it
after you.

The Knowledge

Constellations know all about stars,
Racing drivers understand cars,
Stories know all about blah blah blahs,
But a fist knows how to leave scars.

A cloud knows all about sky,
A fox knows how to be sly,
A newborn baby knows how to cry,
But a bullet knows how to fly.

A roller coaster knows how to thrill,
A refrigerator knows how to chill,
A can of beans knows how to spill,
But a gun understands how to kill.

Rock 'n' rollers know how to jive,
Swarms of bees know all about hives,
Trains know how to depart and arrive,
But a knife knows how to take lives.

Never

Never scarily squared up to a bully in a fight,
Never noisily let loose a Tarzan call at midnight.

Never intentionally labelled someone I know
    a creep,
Never nosily found a secret I couldn't keep.

Never purposely lifted my foot and squashed
    a snail,
Never knowingly whispered love songs
    into the ear of a whale.

Never tidily arranged all my pens in a perfectly
    pleasing row,
Never nervously tiptoed a tightrope with
    a doomsday drop below.

Never ridiculously catalogued and labelled all of
    my dreams,
Never magnificently saved a goal for
    the England football team.

(*In my dreams, maybe.*)

Poems for Performing

My Rock'n'Roll Iguana

A Tribute to Little Richard

My rock'n'roll iguana
Can be heard all down the street,
From New York to San Francisco
His feet tap out the beat.

He's the lizard king of LA
With a twist and a curl of his lip,
A lyrical miracle marvel
Singing songs that are really hip.

Awopbopaloobop Awopbamboom
I'm rocking with my iguana
Awopbopaloobop Awopbamboom
Down at the Club Tropicana

Each night he's in the groove
Break-dancing over the floor.
Every latest dance move
He's ready to explore.

His dexterity is admired
By dancers all around,
His steps are light and nimble
Keeping everyone spellbound.

Awopbopaloobop Awopbamboom
I'm rocking with my iguana
Awopbopaloobop Awopbamboom
Down at the Club Tropicana

And he's found himself a studio
By the beaches of Malibu
And he's really having a blast
Bringing rock'n'roll to you.

He belts out 'Long Tall Sally',
'Tutti Frutti' and 'Teddy Bear',
Completely at home in the spotlight,
A star beneath the glare

Awopbopaloobop Awopbamboom
I'm rocking with my iguana
Awopbopaloobop Awopbamboom
Down at the Club Tropicana

And everyone loves my iguana,
From the Tyrol to Tijuana,
From Bexhill to Botswana,
Even Barrack Obama,
Everyone loves my iguana.....

Awopbopaloobop Awopbamboom,
Awopbopaloobop Awopbamboom,
AWOPBOPALOOBOP AWOPBAMBOOM..........

Back in Those Stone-Age Days

Rock and roll
those rolling stones,
crack-a-crack
those mammoth bones…

Blow that bone flute
toot, toot, toot,
howl and holler,
holler and hoot…

Let's make music like they did before,
back in the old days,
back in the cold days,
back in those stone-age days.

On a row of skulls
beat out a beat.
Play fast and loud,
work up a heat.

Run sticks across
a mammoth's rib cage,
rat-a-tat-tat,
fly into a rage.

Let's make music like they did before,
back in the old days,
back in the cold days,
back in those stone-age days.

Clickety-clack
a woolly rhino's jaws,
rattle the spines
of dinosaurs.

Bash those bones
and whack those molars,
let's be Stone Age
rock'n'rollers.

Making music like they did before,
back in the old days,
back in the cold days,
back in those stone-age days.

In the Stone Age there may have been lots of bones
of dinosaurs to be found and children would have
probably used them as playthings.

Bang a Drum

If you feel like the world
is on your back
and there's nothing that you can do
but attack…

Bang a drum.

If you feel that everyone's
down on you
and you're drowning and wondering
what you can do…

Bang a drum.

When the world looks
such an ugly place,
when you can't see a smile
on anyone's face…

Bang a drum.

Bang a drum,
bang it hard,
let it sound out loud,
let everyone know
you stand out from the crowd.

Let everyone hear
what you have to say,
let them understand
that it's your day today…

Bang a drum.

So don't let others
look down on you.
Be who you are,
know what you can do.
Stand up tall,
be glad, be proud.
Hear that drumbeat,
sound it loud…

Bang a drum.

Bang a drum.
Bang a drum.
BANG A DRUM.

Brian Moses has worked as a professional poet since 1988 and performs his poetry and percussion shows in schools, libraries, theatres and festivals around the UK and abroad. When asked by CBBC to write a poem for the late Queen's 80th birthday he wrote a poem about her corgis. He has published many children's poetry collections, as well as books written with Roger Stevens, including *Olympic Poems, What Are We Fighting For?* and *1066 and Before That*. Brian lives in East Sussex with his wife and their black labrador called Jess. His website is: *www.brianmoses. co.uk* and he blogs at *brian-moses.blogspot.com*

Ed Boxall is an illustrator, writer, performer and educator. He has written and illustrated many picture books such as *Francis the Scaredy Cat* and *Mr Trim and Miss Jumble*. His passion for poetry shows in his illustration work – he has illustrated for some of the UK's top children's poets such as Brian Moses, Roger Stevens and James Carter. Ed's own solo children's poetry collection, *Me and My Alien Friend*, was published in 2018. He performs and runs workshops with children, using an exciting mix of spoken word, projections, giant story books and music. *www.edboxall.com*